IS THERE A LIFE LEFT FOR...

GRANDPARENTS!

BY
TONI GOFFE

HELP

First published in Great Britain by
Pendulum Gallery Press
56 Ackender Road, Alton, Hants GU34 1JS

© TONI GOFFE 1994

IS THERE A LIFE LEFT FOR GRANDPARENTS?
ISBN 0-948912-25-X

PRINTED IN GREAT BRITAIN BY
UNWIN BROTHERS LTD, OLD WOKING, SURREY

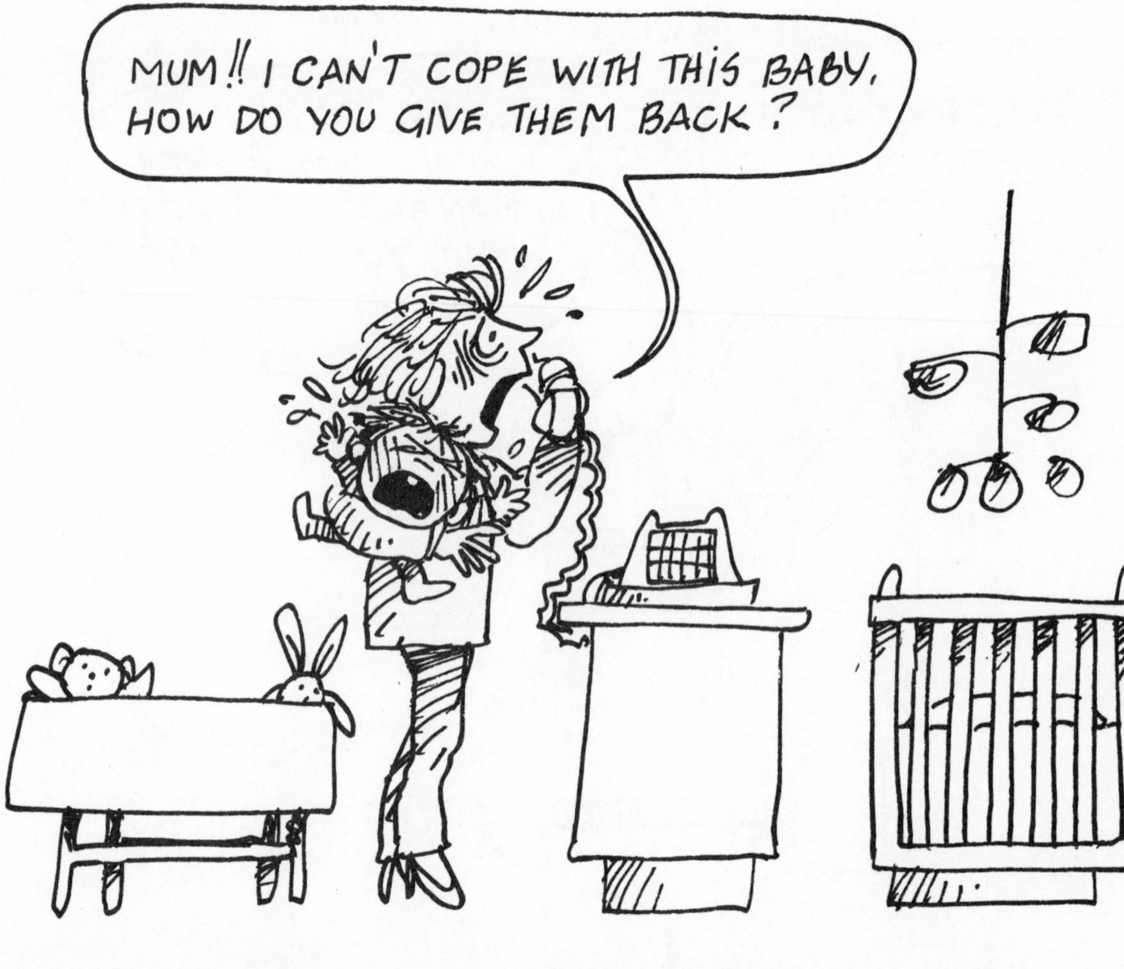
MUM!! I CAN'T COPE WITH THIS BABY.
HOW DO YOU GIVE THEM BACK?

IF I SAY EVERYTHING IS UNDER CONTROL, THEN EVERYTHING IS UNDER CONTROL!

" IT'S ALWAYS THE SAME, WHEN IT'S BEDTIME, YOU CAN NEVER FIND HIM ... "

WE MET BABY SITTING, DIDN'T WE? I DIDN'T THINK WE'D STILL BE DOING IT AT OUR AGE, DID YOU?
AND THE BABY SITTING

A PINT OF BITTER, A WHITE WINE AND COULD YOU WARM THIS UP TO 98·4 DEGREES PLEASE...

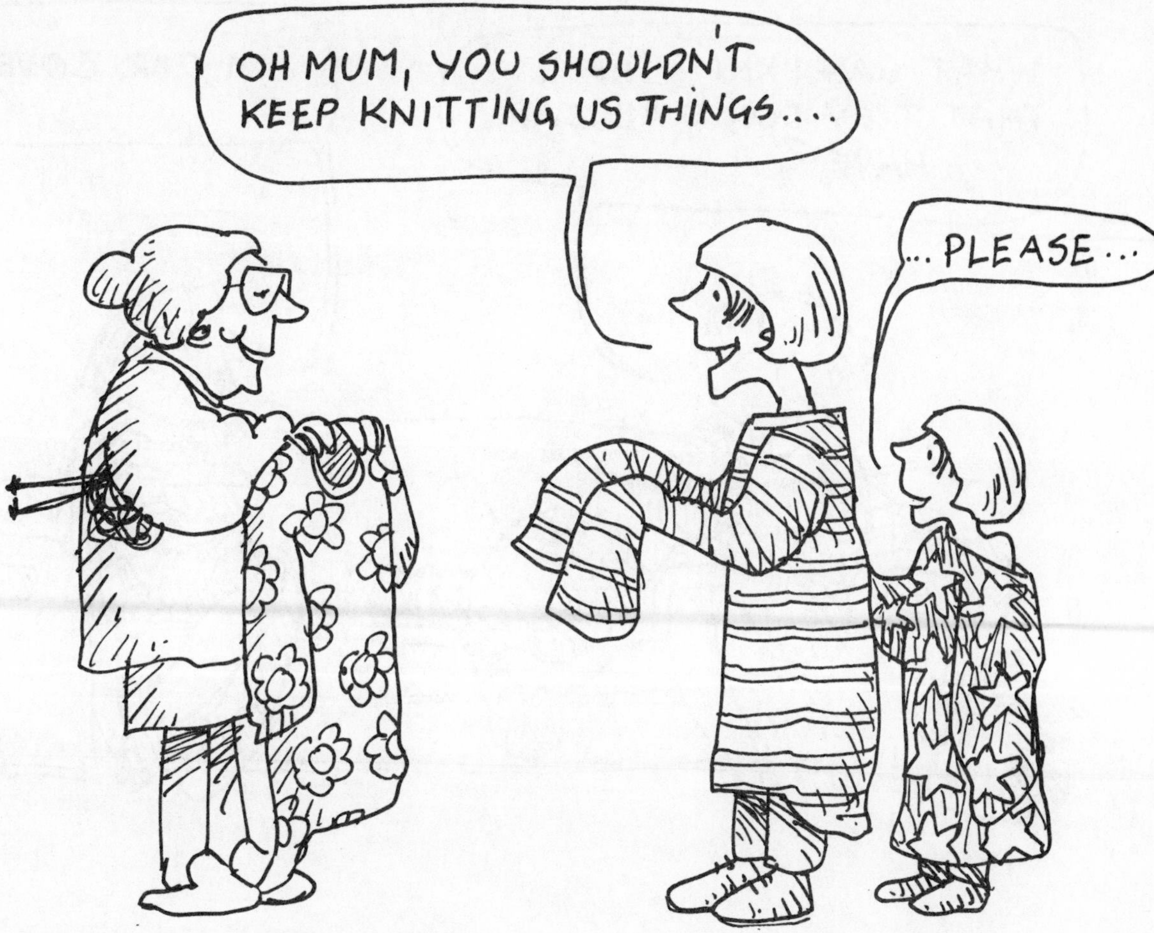
OH MUM, YOU SHOULDN'T KEEP KNITTING US THINGS....
...PLEASE...

HEY GRANDAD, YOU'RE REALLY GOOD FUN — PITY YOU NEVER HAD ANY KIDS OF YOUR OWN...

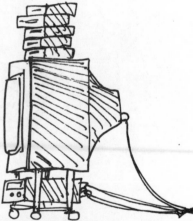

WELL, THAT'S WHAT HE WANTED FOR HIS BIRTHDAY — SO THAT'S WHAT WE GOT HIM...
CONDOMS